CW00523896

THE INDUSTRIAL REVOLUTION

The Birth of the Modern World

Written by Jérémy Rocteur
In collaboration with Thomas Jacquemin
Translated by Rebecca Neal

History **50MINUTES**.com

THE INDUSTRIAL REVOLUTION

KEY INFORMATION

- **When:**
  - The First Industrial Revolution began around 1750 and ended in 1850.
  - The Second Industrial Revolution began around 1870 and ended in 1914.
- **Where:** Europe and the USA.
- **Context:** The increase in population and demand required a higher production rate. To achieve this, improvements had to be made across several sectors, which gradually became mechanised.
- **Key protagonists:**
  - John Kay, British inventor (1704-c. 1780).
  - James Watt, Scottish mechanical engineer (1736-1819).
  - Karl Benz, German engineer (1844-1929).
  - Thomas Edison, American inventor (1847-1931).
- **Impact:**
  - Unprecedented economic changes.
  - Acceleration of demographic growth.
  - The emergence of new social classes.
  - The Third Industrial Revolution.

INTRODUCTION

Since the late 15th century, Europe had been experiencing slow economic growth punctuated by constant crises. However, in England this growth accelerated in the second half of the 18th century thanks to a demographic explosion which would require a higher rate of production. The textile sector was the first to become mechanised, followed by the metallurgy and mining sectors. The changes that took place were so significant that the period is referred to as the Industrial Revolution.

However, the events that took place between this time and the 21st century were not a complete break with the old order. It would be more correct to talk about a phenomenon of industrialisation which had an undeniable impact on human history. For the first time, the means of production of material goods developed across all sectors, profoundly changing the day-to-day lives of individuals.

An essentially agricultural Western society defined by weak growth became an industrial and commercial society characterised by the constant search for improvement with the aim of increasing production capacity. These changes obviously had economic, social, environmental and political consequences. However, far from being a unique and repetitive process, the history of the Industrial Revolution spans several centuries and is still being written today.

CONTEXT

BRITAIN AND THE START OF THE INDUSTRIAL ERA

Since the end of the 17th century, the British population had been growing spectacularly. Unlike in previous centuries, when spikes in the birth rate were accompanied by a high mortality rate, the mortality rate was now gradually decreasing. The population rose from 6 million inhabitants in 1760 to 12 million in 1820. Although this growth provided the agricultural sector with a considerable workforce, there were also more mouths to feed, and this number was rising much more quickly.

With this in mind, and with favourable circumstances on its side, Britain was the first European country to enter the era of industrialisation. This head start on the rest of the continent can be explained by a range of economic, political and societal factors.

A thriving market

Britain's markets, both domestic and foreign, were sizeable and flourishing. Unlike most European countries, Britain had lifted customs duties at the start of the 18th century, which meant that the price of imported products had not increased. This was not an insignificant factor for a country with many colonies from which it could draw the resources needed to produce its goods. Furthermore, British subsoil was rich in raw materials that could easily be exploited.

These included coal and iron, which are indispensable for industry to function effectively. A very developed communication network for the time and the many waterways in the country made it easier to transport them. These waterways were of vital importance: not only did they allow raw materials and products to circulate, but they also made it easier to work the machines.

The country's economy was just as strong. Britain's currency (the pound sterling) could be found on every continent and, in the 19th century, would become the currency of international trade. Finally, the financial and banking networks were concentrated in the heart of London, in the City, further strengthening the economy.

Policies to encourage industrial development

The state would also play an important role in the coming revolution. The British government was responsible for a series of laws encouraging scientific education and industry. Furthermore, it granted a certain degree of autonomy to local decision-makers, who were more aware of the realities and economic needs of their region, which allowed them to take a certain number of decisions to facilitate industrial development.

However, according to the French historian François Cochet (born in 1954), the essential factor in Britain's early entry into the Industrial Revolution is more to do with the political maturity and social openness of the country, which were a result of the revolutions of the 17th century. Indeed, the monarchy was less absolutist than in the rest of Europe, and therefore did not impose its own vision of mercantilism.

17th CENTURY ENGLAND: A PERIOD OF MAJOR UPHEAVAL

The rupture between Parliament and King Charles I (1600-1649) marked the beginning of the first and second English Civil Wars (1642-1649), which culminated in the execution of the king and the proclamation of the Commonwealth, a government led by Oliver Cromwell (Lord Protector of England, Scotland and Ireland, 1599-1658).

In 1660, the monarchy was restored and King James II (1633-1701), who was very authoritarian and a strict Catholic in a mostly Protestant country, acceded to the throne. The tensions that had subsided were quick to reappear and royal prerogatives were reduced following an Act of Parliament. Power was gradually decentralised and the middle classes saw their position in society strengthened, while the landowning aristocracy lost its monopoly on political power. In addition, the adoption of the Bill of Rights in 1689 forbade the raising of taxes unless this was agreed by the national parliament first, and enshrined many individual freedoms, including freedom of speech and the right to petition. This all helped to make English society more individualised and more open, with fewer social groups with codified practices, as was the case elsewhere in Europe.

England's particularly flexible social structure allowed the nobility to invest in industry and new technologies. This meant that a greater spirit of entrepreneurship developed compared with the rest of the continent. The demand of the English middle class, which increased as the tertiary sector (trade, banks and the liberal professions) developed, also contributed to overall growth. Furthermore, the rapid population increase provided businesses with many workers.

Finally, the prevailing economic liberalism of the time drove individuals to try and become rich. Patent law is one of the symbols of this. This law guaranteed inventors a right to a share of the profits arising from the application of their inventions. People's mentalities were therefore completely different on the two sides of the Channel: whereas the French middle class wanted more than anything to become part of the nobility, the English middle class tended to seize the economic opportunities in front of it, which was a less socially gratifying but more profitable approach.

ECONOMIC LIBERALISM

Adam Smith (Scottish economist, 1723-1790) was the thinker behind economic liberalism. In *An Inquiry into the Nature and Causes of the Wealth of Nations* (1776), he analysed economic growth in the 18th century. According to him, economic progress depends on the division of labour, which allows workers to increase their skill level and therefore their productivity. He also recommended expanding markets and laissez-faire economics, which is why his doctrine came to be ter-

Innovations to boost production

While Europe had been experiencing significant technical progress since the 16th century, this progress accelerated spectacularly in Britain over the course of the 18th century. This can be explained in particular by the benefits that patent law brought for inventors, but also by the fact that machines seemed more efficient than an often-undisciplined human workforce, while at the same time enabling better-quality and more regular production.

Research also encouraged the development of new techniques through the critical method it espoused. Unlike earlier traditional learning, where the teachings of religion were simply accepted, scientists were now basing their conclusions on the methodical observation of nature and its phenomena. As such, uneducated researchers and craftspeople embarked on a range of experiments and, in doing so, pushed their experiments further in order to find results that could be used in inventions, without trying to explain these results scientifically. In the hope of resolving specific problems that were slowing down production, they developed new techniques based on the Industrial Revolution that would lead to new innovations.

KEY PROTAGONISTS

JOHN KAY AND THE FLYING SHUTTLE

Portrait of John Kay. There is a flying shuttle on the table in front of him.

John Kay was born in Walmersley (Lancashire) in 1704 to a well-off family of yeoman farmers. After his father died, he left school at the age of 14 to become the apprentice of a weaving loom manufacturer. However, he left this position after just a month of training, claiming that he had learnt everything there was to know about the profession. In spite of this overconfidence that was already one of his distinguishing features, he proved to be a talented inventor. In particular, his inventions led to considerable improvements in weaving, and he filed his first patents in the 1730s.

In 1733, he registered a patent for a new weaving machine which featured his flying shuttle. This machine was lighter than previous models, could be used for weaving wool as well as flax, and allowed work to be carried out faster and with fewer workers. First called a wheeled shuttle, thus emphasising its mobility, then a fly-shuttle, the machine was finally named the flying shuttle. Although Kay's invention made him famous, it was imperfect to start with and needed several years for improvements to be made. In addition, Kay wanted to become rich quickly, and the amount per year he charged to use his machine was so high that many weavers refused to pay it. He then embarked on several court cases, which he lost and which brought him to the brink of ruin.

In spite of his bad-tempered side, many years later a large number of people saw in this invention the genius of the man who has long been considered the founder of the British textile industry. Kay was undeniably a great inventor, and his invention enabled a substantial increase in the quantity of material weaved. This in turn required an improvement in spinning, since there could be no weaving without thread, which finally set off the dynamic of the First Industrial Revolution. Nonetheless, it would be 60 years before his flying shuttle would be established across the entire country.

In 1747, burdened by debt, he was forced to emigrate to France, where he obtained the privilege of being the sole manufacturer and seller of his machines. He died during the winter of 1780-1781 in the south of France.

JAMES WATT AND THE STEAM ENGINE

Portrait of James Watt, painting by Karl Frederik von Breda.

Born in 1736 in Greenock (Scotland), James Watt was a self-taught man with a passion for mechanics. He was introduced to manual labour at a very early age thanks to his father's ship- and house-building business. In 1755, he went to London to learn to make scientific instruments, before returning to Scotland, where he enrolled at the University of Glasgow in 1757. As part of his duties, he was tasked with repairing the steam engine of Thomas Newcomen (English inventor, 1663-1729). He made numerous improvements to the machine, with the financial support of the industrialist John Roebuck (1718-1794) and the chemist Joseph Black (1728-1799), including in particular a modification which aimed to limit the waste of steam produced by the engine. Watt considerably improved the engine's efficiency by using a separate condenser, thus removing the need to regularly cool the engine. Watt was granted a patent for his first engine in 1769 and, from the 1770s onwards, he dedicated all his time to building it, completing the first ones in 1776.

Replica of a stream engine designed by James Watt.

British entrepreneurs then took up Watt's invention and honed it so that it could be adapted to other industrial machines. However, the engine he had designed proved to be too bulky and did not allow enough pressure to power several machines. It was therefore quickly superseded by competition from hydraulic energy. It was not until the improvements made by Richard Trevithick (British engineer, 1771-1833) that the engine became powerful enough to be used in steamboats and trains.

James Watt died in Heathfield in 1819, at the age of 83.

DID YOU KNOW?

The watt, a unit of power, is named after James Watt in recognition of his work.

KARL BENZ AND THE INTERNAL-COMBUSTION ENGINE

Portrait of Karl Benz.

Born in 1844 in Karlsruhe, Baden-Württemberg (Germany), Karl Benz was still a child when his father died. At a very young age he began working to help his mother and support them, which is why he began repairing watches and clocks.

Thanks to his inclination for technical subjects, he was able to study engineering at the polytechnic university in Karlsruhe. He specialised in engine design, with the dream of developing a car which could move without being drawn by horses or powered by steam. Believing he had learnt enough, he opened his own engine workshop in Mannheim and managed to attract a number of investors. With their financial backing, he founded a new company, which he hoped would allow him to produce the engine he had dreamed about for so long. However, although the company was profitable, his shareholders were not prepared to follow him in this venture, which they judged to be too risky. He therefore decided to leave the factory.

In 1883, with the support of new investors, he founded his third company, which he named Benz & Cie. after himself. The new shareholders now supported him in his car-making project. Two years later, his dream finally became a reality, when he developed a motorised three-wheeled vehicle, the first horseless carriage powered by an internal-combustion engine. This was a genuine revolution, as since the start of the century and until that point all self-propelled vehicles had been powered by steam engines. Benz's model proved to be much more compact and, above all, much more efficient. The invention was enthusiastically welcomed and seemed to have a bright future ahead of it. And rightly so: many consider Benz's motorised vehicle to be the first automobile in history.

Benz's motorised vehicle, unveiled in 1888.

However, another German inventor, Gottlieb Daimler (1834-1900), had patented an internal-combustion engine a few months earlier. He was therefore the original inventor of the first motorised vehicle and, as a result, Benz's main competitor. This led to intense rivalry on the French and German markets. In the interests of marketing, Daimler called his car Mercedes, a French-sounding name that was likely to appeal to more people.

After the First World War (1914-1918), Germany sank into an economic depression. To deal with this difficult situation, the two rival companies decided to merge under the name Mercedes-Benz in 1926. Following this merger, Karl Benz, by now an old man, stepped down from the head of his factory but remained on the board until his death.

THOMAS EDISON AND THE INCANDESCENT BULB

Photograph of Thomas Edison posing with his incandescent bulb.

Thomas Edison was born in Milan, Ohio in 1847. After spending only three months at school, he was taught entirely by his mother. From the age of 12, he began a series of small jobs such as fruit seller, newspaper boy and telegraph operator.

He was an astute observer, and his experience as a telegraphist allowed him to make improvements to his work tool. After patenting his first inventions and pocketing a tidy sum, he surrounded himself with a team of chemists, physicists and mathematicians to collaborate on research for new inventions. At the start of the 1870s, his activity became very profitable. In particular, he perfected the telegraph, the typewriter and the telephone, before selling his inventions to large companies. With the aim of surrounding himself with the best scientists, his company grew and, in just a few short years, over 300 patents were filed.

One of his most profitable and original inventions was without doubt the phonograph, which he registered the patent for in 1877. The basic device allowed sounds to be impressed onto a sheet of metal, so that they could then be played. In a few years, he managed to considerably improve this machine and its apparatus, filing no fewer than 80 patents for this work.

However, the invention he is most commonly associated with is the incandescent bulb. After testing thousands of metallic and organic fibres to find the best possible filament, Edison settled on Japanese bamboo. Immediately, a large number of low-cost bulbs were produced and, thanks to them, Edison helped to set up the first power stations. This hugely important invention would light up the world and bring fame and fortune to its inventor. Other inventions of his would bring about major changes in the world, in particular the electric chair and the kinetograph, the first camera in history. Edison died at the age of 84, leaving behind over a thousand patents.

DID YOU KNOW?

Thomas Edison was a complete workaholic. It was not unusual for him to only sleep for four hours per night, or to work for 50 hours straight. There was a good reason for this: when he was working on a new invention, he wanted to know everything there was to know about the subject.

THE INDUSTRIAL REVOLUTION

THE FIRST INDUSTRIAL REVOLUTION (1750-1850)

The term 'revolution' is not used in its traditional sense here. Indeed, there was not an initial state of economic stagnation followed suddenly by a period rich in innovations which led to industrial breakthroughs. Rather, Western countries had been experiencing slow economic growth punctuated by crises since the end of the Middle Ages. This growth then accelerated at the end of the 18th century, when new procedures appeared and were gradually adopted.

Britain leads the way

The First Industrial Revolution took place in Britain, where there was a very favourable context for these changes. Since the late 17th century, spectacular population growth meant that it had been necessary to produce more to support the population. Consequently, starting in the 18th century, many inventions appeared, particularly in the textile and metallurgy sectors, where it had been necessary to resolve specific problems that were slowing down production. As a consequence of these new advances, complementary activities developed and their mechanisms were improved as they in turn embarked on industrialisation.

Cotton spinning was one of the first sectors to become mechanised, and many consider this to be the driving force behind all industrialisation in Britain. Its mechanisation began in the mid-18th century with machines such as John Kay's flying shuttle, which made weaving quicker. Consequently, the demand for spun cotton increased, and it was therefore also necessary to improve spinning so as to prevent bottlenecks in production. In the same way, other activities in the chain of production, such as bleaching, had to be perfected in turn in order to cope with demand, and so on. Next, innovations in the metallurgy sector appeared. These used new sources of energy such as steam, which was produced by burning a new fuel that would come to symbolise the First Industrial Revolution: coal.

This production increase was accompanied by the modernisation of transport. Initially, this was achieved thanks to investment from the state, which saw the longed-for opportunity to develop exchange and in this way boost trade. The baton was then passed to private companies. The First Industrial Revolution involved above all the modernisation of old transport routes, canals, ports and roads. At the same time, a new means of transport appeared: the railway. From 1800 onwards, passenger trains appeared in England, but they were still pulled by animals. With the development of T-Tracks and the first steam locomotives, a first line was opened to the public between Manchester and Liverpool in 1830. Although its initial average speed was just 15 mph, this, along with trains' transport capacity, would increase very quickly.

Official opening of the railway line between Manchester and Liverpool, 1830.

Although a number of innovations emerged in the manufacturing and transport sectors, these did not completely replace traditional methods. As such, by the mid-19th century, the most commonly-used engine in Europe and the USA was still the water mill. This meant that old forms of power (human, animal and hydraulic) were preserved, while at the same time new techniques and energy sources were being developed. This complementarity could also be seen in the forms of work organisation at this time. While there was a kind of resistance to proto-industry in mainland Europe, this system rapidly became unstructured in Britain. Agriculture therefore developed in large and small operations, as well as tenant farms, where mechanisation allowed the costlier workforce to be replaced. Elsewhere in Europe, entrepreneurs were very attached to crafts because, unlike factory workers, craftspeople had no social requirements. Entrepreneurs therefore played on the complementarity between these two systems and the advantages they offered in terms of organisation of work: mechanisation was used for mass production, whereas crafts remained useful for more individualised orders.

The changes in manufacturing processes were so great that they can be described as a revolution. It is true that society underwent major changes: one century after the start of the Industrial Revolution, almost 50% of the British population worked in industry and was now living in urban areas. As a whole, the workers provided 20% of industrial goods worldwide, including in particular half the iron and cotton clothing and two thirds of the coal used across the world.

Part of Europe lags behind

The situation proved more complex in the rest of Europe, where the revolution was slower to take root. Power in these countries was more centralised and the state often played a greater role than in Britain. Private initiative was also weaker and the industrialist policies implemented by the central authorities were often unsuited to the reality on the ground. Furthermore, some entrepreneurs tried to mechanise heavy industry, such as metallurgy, as a matter of priority, whereas Britain had tackled the textile industry first. The lack of a sufficiently large middle class was also one of the main causes of this delay. France is the best example of this: peasants, who represented the largest class in French society, could not afford to purchase the new manufactured products.

The process was different in each country. In some regions, and unlike in Britain, there was no leading sector capable of bringing about the rest of industrialisation, as was the case with the textile industry across the Channel. Some then tried to develop mechanisation in all sectors at once, which did not necessarily respond to the reality of the situation or to the country's economic needs. Others, such as Belgium, attempted to imitate and adapt British techniques, but many difficulties arose. Indeed, this required expertise that only British workers possessed. In addition, technological transfers were limited, because England did not allow skilled workers to emigrate or machines to be exported until the mid-19th century. However, this did not stop a number of skilled workers and labourers from moving to mainland Europe to set up their own businesses. While they waited for their nascent modern industries to develop enough to become competitive, many countries decided to protect them by imposing high customs barriers on British products.

France, Germany and Belgium industrialised at the start of the 19th century and, by 1840, reached the same technical level as Britain. France even encouraged scientific competition and developed its education system by teaching mechanics. Germany, strengthened following its unification (1871), did the same and saw rapid industrial growth. Belgium embarked on the Industrial Revolution from 1830 onwards and, thanks to its steel, mining and textile industries and to major investments in its rail networks, soon joined the ranks of the great industrial nations.

Conversely, other parts of Europe did not experience a real industrial boom. This was the case for Russia – in spite of some pockets of industrialisation shortly before the First World War – and for Mediterranean countries. Indeed, unlike Italy, which experienced significant industrialisation at the end of the 19th century, Spain and Portugal had not enjoyed agricultural modernisation beforehand. In addition, there were no fundamental social changes, which are the source of a degree of political maturity necessary for industrialisation. These countries found themselves financially dependent on England, which means that they remained supplier countries for staple products, such as wine.

The rest of the world

Western Europe and the USA seem to be the only parts of the world to have experienced a real industrial revolution at this time. Nonetheless, the beginnings of modern industry developed in other regions, such as South America and the Ottoman Empire, but without ever reaching the proportions observed in the Western world. In spite of their desire to catch up with the West through state industrialisation policies, there were many obstacles, especially on the social level. The majority of the population in these countries lived in poverty. In addition, the small elite was resistant to change which could challenge its social predominance. Merchants, financiers and craftspeople therefore remained subject to the emperor, the caliph or whoever else held central power. If they did manage to manufacture products, they were dependent on foreign markets, which they needed to sell their products as the domestic market was too weak to absorb them. The Western countries were in a position of strength and forced these countries to adopt a liberal trade policy which undid all their efforts to gain autonomy.

THE UNIQUE CASE OF JAPAN

For a long time, Japan had been one of the most closed-off countries in the world. Nonetheless, in the 19th century the Europeans forced it to open up and subjected it to a series of unequal treaties. To fight against this, Emperor Meiji (1852-1912) decided to beat the westerners at their own game, namely industrialisation, through the steel industry, thanks to iron mines and the blast furnaces that appeared in the first half of the 19th century. This was followed by a forced modernisation of the country, which underwent a number of social reforms that primarily affected the old feudal elite. Their land rent was quickly transferred to the state, which developed economically by increasing food production and launched an efficient textile industry. At the same time, Japan tried to attract skilled workers from the West by offering them a tempting salary, while sending many Japanese students to learn in the best universities in Europe. As it was unable to apply protectionist tariffs on foreign countries following treaties which favoured the West, Japanese industry made the most of this to constantly seek new innovations.

THE SECOND INDUSTRIAL REVOLUTION (1870-1914)

During the second half of the 19th century, the situation developed. A new generation of inventors came along and started the Second Industrial Revolution. From now on, highly qualified scientists replaced hands-on craftspeople and applied the results of their research to the needs of universities, countries and industry.

Furthermore, production decreased from 1870 onwards, notably following the various crises at that time, but also because supply had become too high compared with demand. Two young nations, Germany and the USA, then became more important and started to produce more than Britain. In the last three decades of the 19th century, their growth rate doubled compared with that of Great Britain.

New inventions were unveiled and a new material that was more resistant and more malleable than iron appeared: steel. Although scientists had known how to make it for centuries, it had not been considered until now because the process was particularly expensive. However, in the late 19th century, techniques which allowed large quantities of steel to be produced for the same price as iron were developed. Steel then became the base of all the new machines and technologies. Germany was a major manufacturer of steel, and by the eve of the First World War it was producing almost as much as France, England, Italy and Russia combined.

The close of the century was also marked by the emergence

of new forms of energy. There was a good reason for this: the steam engine seemed to have reached the limit of its potential. This machine, which was both highly polluting and bulky, was gradually replaced by internal-combustion engines which required fewer human resources, could work at different rhythms and speeds, and could be started and stopped more easily. This new invention was primarily used in the automobile sector. Furthermore, an increasing number of cities were lit up at night thanks to the development and spread of electricity.

The main beneficiary of the Second Industrial Revolution was the USA. At the dawn of the 20th century, it was producing more automobiles than the rest of the world combined and was the leading producer in almost all sectors (metallurgy, chemicals, etc.) thanks to a new approach to industrial production based on a scientific organisation of work where each individual was responsible for a clearly defined stage in the process, allowing greater mass production than in the past.

WAS THERE REALLY A SECOND INDUSTRIAL REVOLUTION?

This question is still being debated by historians. It has been noted that a new generation of highly qualified scientists who based their inventions on applied knowledge appeared from the 1870s onwards. New inventions also emerged, but it sometimes took decades for their true applications to materialise. For example, Zénobe Gramme (Belgian electrical engineer and inventor, 1826-1901) filed a patent for a direct current machine in 1869, whereas electricity only really became useable when Thomas Edison developed the incandescent lightbulb ten years later. Consequently, some historians see the Second Industrial Revolution as merely an extension of the first. Indeed, there was no energy revolution comparable to the one which brought coal to power thanks to the steam engine. Only the automobile was really a part of the dynamic of industrialisation, with its internal-combustion engine which replaced the steam engine. Meanwhile, coal would remain the main energy source until the 1920s.

IMPACT

THE ECONOMY BECOMES GLOBAL

The many changes in transport and the development of a maritime network (digging of the Suez Canal in 1863 and the Panama Canal in 1914) allowed enormous quantities of goods to be transported for greater distances. Trade expanded and the economy became increasingly globalised.

These changes led to a new business concept: limited companies, which limited the responsibility of their members to their investments alone, proliferated, and companies joined together to form consortiums, cartels, trusts and other holdings. There was also an increasing number of merchant banks, and in large cities commodity exchanges (trading of goods already produced, in production and to be produced) and stock exchanges (trading of bonds and shares) appeared.

It is also worth noting that, contrary to popular belief, large factories were still rare in the 19th century. Indeed, in the second half of the century, companies had on average ten employees. The concentration of the workforce only progressed very slowly. Finally, the Industrial Revolution changed the face of economic crises: previously, these were characterised by underproduction, but now they took the form of crises of overproduction.

THE DEVELOPMENT OF THE ARMAMENTS INDUSTRY

In 1914, on the eve of the First World War, the Western industrial powers controlled over 80% of the world's territories. Technology from civilian industry had found plenty of applications in the armaments industry. The precision and recharge speed of guns and the power of explosives were constantly improving. Steam power and electricity were followed by the power to kill. The First World War provided a bloody demonstration of the progress made in weaponry in the space of a century.

MAJOR DEMOGRAPHIC CHANGES

Demographic growth accelerated in industrialised countries in the 19th centuries, following an increase in the life expectancy of the upper classes thanks to medicine, which had also taken significant steps forward. The Industrial Revolution therefore also led to unprecedented population growth and a level of urbanisation and pollution that were previously unknown in the history of humanity.

However, in the first few years, the Industrial Revolution initially led to a considerable reduction in life expectancy, particularly among the working classes. It took a long time for scientists to understand that people's health and sanitary conditions were linked to this phenomenon. It was thanks to improved research techniques in particular that the causes of many illnesses could be identified. Synthesis chemistry was developed during the Second Industrial

Revolution. At the start of the 19th century, the first medicines appeared and new fertilisers to boost agricultural output were produced, among other developments.

Apart from Great Britain, all societies were predominantly rural until the mid-19th century. However, the agricultural sector was becoming weaker due to the draining effect of industrialisation and urbanisation on the people in the countryside. Migration towards the towns, which was initially gradual and often temporary, accelerated and intensified with industrialisation, which ruined rural crafts, beginning with textiles. The town attracted workers and kept them in factories. Between 1851 and 1910-1914, the percentage of urban dwellers rose from 48 to 73% in Great Britain, 25.5 to 44.2% in France, 7.8% to 19.6% in Russia and around 11 to 45.7% in the USA.

Moreover, industrialisation and the transport revolution led to the huge expansion of population centres and above all the formation of large cities with over a million inhabitants. Towns spread past their outer walls, extended towards the outskirts along the axes of communication, and grew upwards in the centre. Within them, there was social segregation, with the wealthy in the nicest neighbourhoods and the poorest confined to the deprived and industrial areas on the outskirts.

THE BOOM IN EMIGRATION IN THE 19TH CENTURY

The 19th century also saw a boom in emigration. The major migratory movements were intercontinental and involved above all Europeans, around 40 million of whom emigrated to America. The main reason for leaving was poverty caused by structural changes and the periodic crises which affected their home countries. In addition, there was the attraction of the host countries (the USA, Canada, Brazil, Argentina and Australia), which promised fame and fortune.

REORGANISATION OF THE SOCIAL ORDER

The working class

The material conditions of the working class are difficult to describe. Wages varied between regions and factories. In some cases, owners took it upon themselves to look after their workers. They embarked on workforce management policies to keep skilled workers in their factories thanks to a series of benefits, offering housing, schools and retirement payments. They also closely watched and monitored the morality of their employees, whose lives were almost entirely governed by their employer.

However, with the profusion of workers leaving the countryside, working conditions quickly deteriorated: the working day was often over 12 hours long, child labour became more frequent (this would not be regulated by any legislation until 1850), and owners were constantly trying to increase production. They would be helped in this by the emergence of electricity, which allowed working at night to become commonplace.

As well as these difficult working conditions, employees' living conditions were frequently miserable. The mass rural exodus had resulted in overpopulation in the cities. Unfettered urbanisation in industrial areas considerably reduced the quality of life: there was no overall plan to welcome the working population, there was not enough space and the air was polluted by coal smoke. Consequently, public health declined and the mortality rate among workers increased, especially as epidemics ravaged the towns. There was besides these one more problem: alcoholism, the social scourge of the modern era.

Eisenwalzwerk, Iron Rolling Mill, painting by the German artist Adolph Menzel depicting working conditions in the late 19th century.

The business class and the aristocracy

The business class appeared with the Industrial Revolution. Its boldness, success and financial power resulting from the emergence of industrialisation allowed it to play a greater part in political decisions. However, it was increasingly in conflict with the working class and these tensions escalated in the late 19th century. Industrialists used mechanisation to keep salaries low, which had disastrous consequences for workers. The demand for workers decreased and their poverty only grew. Unable to find work, many saw emigration as a way out of their difficulties.

The aristocracy preserved its social prestige thanks to its landholdings. Nonetheless, its political power was weakened. Indeed, 18th-century aristocrats had more trust in traditional investments than in new and highly risky activities such as modern industry.

THE THIRD INDUSTRIAL REVOLUTION

To distinguish each industrial revolution, historians have often assumed coherence between forms of energy, materials, transport techniques and techniques in the consumer sectors. From this point of view, the First Industrial Revolution was embodied by the steam engine, coal, railways and the textile industries, while the second resulted from the interconnection between steel, electricity, synthesis chemistry, automobile and fossil fuels.

For some, the Second Industrial Revolution has not yet finished, and will not be over until humanity moves away from fossil fuels (meaning non-renewable energy sources). Once this is done, the Third Industrial Revolution, which will probably be marked by green energy, will be able to begin. For others, this new revolution will by marked by nanotechnology, biotechnology, information technology and cognitive science (NBIC), opening up almost unlimited possibilities for humanity. Still others believe that the Third Industrial Revolution has already taken place and involves the developments in information technology which began in the 1980s. This last group think that the Third Industrial Revolution is starting already, with the democratisation of 3D printers and open source software, which make the tools of production available to everyone.

One thing is certain: the Industrial Revolution which began at the end of the 18th century has established a society based on a constant need for growth and progress, which is a long way from being finished.

SUMMARY

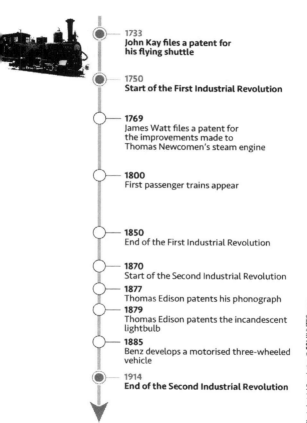

1733
**John Kay files a patent for
his flying shuttle**

1750
Start of the First Industrial Revolution

1769
James Watt files a patent for
the improvements made to
Thomas Newcomen's steam engine

1800
First passenger trains appear

1850
End of the First Industrial Revolution

1870
Start of the Second Industrial Revolution

1877
Thomas Edison patents his phonograph

1879
Thomas Edison patents the incandescent
lightbulb

1885
Benz develops a motorised three-wheeled
vehicle

1914
End of the Second Industrial Revolution

- Britain was the first European country to become industrialised in the late 18th century thanks to its more pronounced growth. There were various factors behind this, including spectacular increases in the population and consumer demand, and the technical expertise and capital necessary for its development.
- Inventors played an important role. To begin with, they were amateurs who tried to improve the tools they had at their disposal through observation and experimentation. The Second Industrial Revolution saw the emergence of highly qualified scientists who based their inventions on applied knowledge.
- Throughout the 19th century, industrialisation spread across Western Europe and reached the USA, which became the world's foremost industrial power at the start of the following century.
- The Industrial Revolution had a range of consequences which affected all sections of society.
- Two new social classes appeared at the dawn of the First World War: the working class, which lived hand-to-mouth, and the business class, which played an increasing part in political decisions. The gap between the lower levels (the workers) and the higher levels (the middle classes) of society grew, while social tensions became increasingly violent.
- With the progress made across all domains, and in particular transport, agriculture and medicine, the population of industrialised countries grew spectacularly.
- Although some think that the Second Industrial Revolution will only end when we abandon fossil fuels, others believe that the Third Industrial Revolution

has already begun and involves the development of information technology. In any case, the society which was established by the First Industrial Revolution and is characterised by the constant drive for progress is far from over.

We want to hear from you!
Leave a comment on your online library
and share your favourite books on social media!

FIND OUT MORE

BIBLIOGRAPHY

- Barnett, D. (1998) *London: Hub of the Industrial Revolution*. London: Tauris Academic Studies.
- Beauchamp, C. (1997) *Révolution industrielle et croissance économique au XIXe siècle*. Paris: Ellipses.
- Cochet, F. and Henry, G. (1995) *Les révolutions industrielles. Processus historiques. Développements économiques*. Paris: Armand Colin.
- Farr, J.R. (2003) *World Eras: Industrial Revolution in Europe (1750-1914)*. New York: Thomson/Gale.
- Horn, J. (2007) *The Industrial Revolution*. London: Greenwood Press.
- Meignen, L. (1996) *Histoire de la révolution industrielle et du développement. 1776-1914*. Paris: PUF.
- Merriman, J. and Winter, J. (2006) *Europe from 1789 to 1914: Encyclopedia of the Age of Industry and Empire*. New York: Charles Scribner's Sons.
- Morris, C.R. (2012) *The Dawn of Innovation: The First American Industrial Revolution*. Philadelphia: Public Affairs.
- Rioux, J.-P. (1971) *La révolution industrielle. 1780-1880*. Paris: Seuil.
- Stearns, P.N. (2013) *The Industrial Revolution in World History*. Boulder, Colorado: Westview Press.
- Verley, P. (2006) *La première révolution industrielle*. Paris: Armand Colin.

ADDITIONAL SOURCES

- Anderson, C. (2013) *Makers: The New Industrial Revolution*. London: Random House Business Books.
- Griffin, E. (2014) *Liberty's Dawn: A People's History of the Industrial Revolution*. New Haven, Connecticut: Yale University Press.
- Mokyr, J. (2011) *The Enlightened Economy: Britain and the Industrial Revolution, 1700-1850*. London: Penguin.
- Osborne, R. (2014) *Iron, Steam & Money: The Making of the Industrial Revolution*. London: The Bodley Head.
- Rifkin, J. (2013) *The Third Industrial Revolution: How Lateral Power is Transforming Energy, the Economy, and the World*. London: Palgrave Macmillan.

ICONOGRAPHIC SOURCES

- Portrait of John Kay. There is a flying shuttle on the table in front of him. Royalty-free reproduction picture.
- *Portrait of James Watt*, painting by Karl Frederik von Breda. Royalty-free reproduction picture.
- Replica of a stream engine designed by James Watt. © Nicolas Perez.
- Portrait of Karl Benz. Royalty-free reproduction picture.
- Benz's motorised vehicle, unveiled in 1888. Royalty-free reproduction picture.
- Photograph of Thomas Edison posing with his incandescent bulb. Royalty-free reproduction picture.
- Official opening of the railway line between Manchester and Liverpool, 1830. Royalty-free reproduction picture.
- *Eisenwalzwerk*, Iron Rolling Mill, painting by the German

artist Adolph Menzel depicting working conditions in the late 19th century. Royalty-free reproduction picture.

DOCUMENTARIES

- *What the Industrial Revolution Did for Us*. (2003) [Documentary series]. Simon Baker, Jonathan Hassid, Billie Pink. Dirs. UK: British Broadcasting Corporation.
- *Capitalism*. (2014) [Documentary]. Ilan Ziv. Dir. France/Canada: Film Option International, Tamouz Media, Zadig Productions.

Printed in Great Britain
by Amazon

72389993R00027